Role Model

What would your life be without a House-wife?

Divya Kotak

BookLeaf Publishing

India | USA | UK

Made with ❤ on the BookLeaf Publishing Platform
www.bookleafpub.in
www.bookleafpub.com

Dedication

To my mother, my Aunt, my Nani and to all the house-wives in this world.

I am a Daughter who grew mostly amongst the women around me.

To my mother, she doesn't know the impact she has in my life. All my Life she has been a person who was present regardless how tired she was. She was the one who gave her ears to me when I wanted to be heard regardless of how many times she went unheard, unappreciated, disrespected. She made sure her daughter would never feel the pain of not being heard. When she needed her family the most they abandoned her emotionally. She was fighting with her inner demons every day but is the purest Angel in my life. My father is the breadwinner of our family yet if ever asked, for me she is the actual provider of our house. we live in a house but with her in it I feel like I am at Home.

My mother became that voice for me. When I was scared to speak up or talk to my father she became my voice and spoke up for me. I come from a family where women after marriage aren't allowed to work. To all the daughters and going to be a daughter-in law of my family. I wish you will fight for your opinions and always chase the purpose you once found.

I hope you would never let something like this stop you from becoming someone you dream of.

I hope in this world for once you all would think for yourself, live for yourself and worry about yourself.

Preface

How did she end up in a place she didn't know?

She dedicated herself to the people she didn't know because that's what she was taught. She was always an avid wanderer living her life with the rules designed by the society. She was naive enough to let the purpose of her life fly away wrapped up in a paper rocket. People expected her to settle. She expected herself to accept. Beginning her journey with hope and excitement to find peace on the other hand with new people while struggling all her life to create a heaven for the people she barely knew. She learnt the concept of give and take through schooling which later she realized was applicable within a limited boundary. As hard as it was for her to find the talent people often used to talk about she had to give it up all to be a housewife. She played the role of a daughter in law, wife and mother at the price of losing her identity altogether. The irony is when she asked for a simple thankyou she was judged for her audacity to be upfront. The society was never ready for a fierce housewife and when they saw one they knew their worst fears were about to come true.

To my Role Models.

To the House makers.

To the women who became the House-wife at some point with or without their will.

Acknowledgements

I would like to give my regards to all the women who have lost themselves a little everyday for their family.
The reason this book even exist in the first place is because of the sacrifices you made for us.
Thankyou for making our lives a little more comfortable, safe and happy.

To the people for making it possible for someone like me to publish this book. If it was not for the Bookleaf Publishing, the idea of seeing my name on the cover would have just been a dream. Thankyou for coming out with a writing challenge to let the writers all around India become the Author they dreamed off.

Thankyou to the people around me who have been a great influence in my life. Being a quiet personality it has often been hard for me to confess my feelings for how grateful I am to have you in my life. I consider myself the most luckiest person alive for the people I have in my life.

To the Readers thankyou for taking out some time from your on going life to read them (housewives).
wherever I am in my life they will always be at the back of mind.
Like Billie Eilish once said,
I see her in the back of my mind all the time,
Like a fever, like I am burning alive.
the question for you my dear Readers is,
Do you see her in the back of your mind?

1. Thicker Than Blood

It took everything in her to not be,
What everyone asked her to be.
She lived for ages,
Betraying her own blood.
Turning out to be the person,
Cursing her inner thrud.

2. An Outsider

Begging for a home,
While desperately wandering around.
Feeling like an outsider
Even between them.
Love is a different game.
While they have been sleeping with love,
I am fighting with my pillows,
Hugging and weeping the beige,
It is overwhelming seeing love pouring like honey,
Like them I too want to taste that feeling.
Sitting under a thick roof,
I still feel homeless.
People around me feel like strangers.
Calling me a silent goof,
When my heart can barely stop.
Sometimes I feel sad for people who are so loved,
They undermine the fact that they are lucky.
They don't realize they have an entire garden,
Where I am looking for just a garland.

3. Choices you made

I lived in your nest,
to be around you.
You were scared to leave your nest,
Abandoning our emotions was your choice.
In your dark web,
She was our photon.
You demanded love,
She defined love.
You betrayed her,
She stood there utterly broke,
You escaped the conversations.
She made sure we have one.
You broke us,
She made us.
You accused her for turning us against you.
When it was you.
It has always been you;

4. She was wrong

I was seeing you from her eyes,
When you were hitting her nerves,
My eyes cried.
When she picked herself,
My heart felt restricted.
When she fought back,
My legs were glued.
When you were having your can,
She listened to you being disrespectful again.
She chose you every time,
Ignoring her colors,
She chose to paint your walls.
You expected her to have some shame,
When she glorified her courage.
Standing up to you was her long lost dream,
When she found her little piece,
When you act like a fool,
She treated you like a jewel.
Denying was inadmissible in her life.
Knowing that you pushed her buttons.
You abused her silence,
Every time i thought you were wrong ,
Your absurdity prolonged.
Being with you was wrong,

Letting you in her life was wrong,
Staying with you was wrong,
Giving you a second chance was wrong,
Maybe She was wrong.

5. For the First Time

For the first time,
I don't feel her pain.
Everything she is holding onto,
is going down the drain.
For the first time,
I want to be selfish,
I want to pick me over her emotions.
Sitting at an edge,
Waiting to be punished,
Drowning in her pain,
Hiding from me,
Lying behind the doors.
She is waiting for her death.
For the first time,
I am considering her thoughts.
Questioning my Identity,
I am horrified by my thoughts.
Thinking death might feel more lively,
and just for a moment,
She might find her ecstasy.
Realizing how worthless I am,
How devastated she might be.
Longing for her presence,
While waiting on the shore,

For our forever.
For the first time,
I don't feel her pain.
Everything she is holding onto,
its going down the drain.

6. How can she be this naive?

Dragging her through their mud,
Polishing her beliefs with their false paint,
Using her trust,
Asking for her promise,
Using her compromises.
How can she be this naive?
Falling for their hypocrisy.
On asking she said,
That's what love is.
In order to find love,
You need to go through these tests.
It's an investment to have a forever.
I couldn't help but laugh.
Are you sure that's love?
Where you have to humiliate your beliefs,
Where you have to bend your morals,
Where you have to keep your opinions in check,
Isn't love a feeling of being home?
The home she was decorating,
Was a house she was living in.
How can she be this naive?

7. I wish I wasn't here

Things aren't that bad,
But i feel horribly sad.
Watching people having each other,
I miss enjoying my own company.
Stuck with the people around.
Carrying their attitudes.
Taking it slow,
letting them win.
Dreaming for paradise,
living in a cage.
I feel distant watching them,
Laughing together,
Crying together.
having their small moments,
entangled together.
I miss my dream,
Waking up every Single Day,
I wish I wasn't here.
I wish I wasn't here.

8. A love story made by the Society

Every morning she wakes up,
Called by the place,
The only place who values her the most.
A place who obeys her Queen.
A place that feels her burns,
A place that glorifies her sweat.
Ladies and gentlemen,
This is a love story of a housewife and her kitchen.
A love so profound.
A love so engaging.
From driving each other nuts,
To protect each other from their edges.
One with sharp blades,
Other with her intense emotions.
They share silence,
Filled with broken promises.
A place she is tired of visiting every day,
Is a place she feels incomplete without.
A place she abuses a lot,
Ends up being a place who welcomes her with an open
arm.
A place built for her.
A relation with a tag,

A relation born from a societal image,
A relation being eyed upon.
A relation which became gender biased.
A love so profound,
Built on an unseen ground,
Walking on a patchy surface,
For some its an illuminated lights,
For some its a silent void.
As toxic as it gets,
One is a lost cause without another.
A love so profound.
A relation so desperate.

9. Blaming and Craving

It's one of those days,
The cage inside me is opening up,
I can see him looking up,
While standing there holding the bars,
Scaring me, he is coming for a war.
It's one of those days.
Hallucinations are taking its peak,
My stars are ruining me,
Locked up for years,
Ready to take a plunge,
I can hear his blood curdling screams.
The thing that's been hidden inside,
It's popping out.
My emotions are breaking the wall,
Powerless and hopeless,
I feel exposed.
Breaking the wall running and gasping.
The more I ran away from him,
The closer it brought me to him.
Tears are at the brim,
Forming cloudy judgements.
Refusing to pull me out.
Cursing me for loving my Loneliness.
Petrified I want to break that bleak void.

It's one of those days.
While still blaming the hands I am living with,
I am out craving for the other hand,
Hoping to pull me out of their manic isolation.
Asking him to lock my demon inside,
Begging him to help me this once,
To help her get away from herself (Demon)
To help her get closer to herself (Dream)

10. When a Wife becomes a Mother

Anxious around her In-laws
Opinionated in front of her children
A scared wife turned into a tough mother.
Relatives called her quiet,
Neighbours commented with their looks.
A place that ought to be her home,
Turned to be a restless zone.
Leaving all her expectations,
She lived for her blood.
Aware of her role as a mother,
We became an added bonus.
A bonus she loved from her soul.
With every single passing day,
When we were compromised by the family,
She began compromising herself.
A role she was meant to step into,
Ended up being a Role Model.

11. Letter from her Mother

It wasn't easy to love you,
I hate myself for saying that.
Selfish I was,
For thinking,
You will make it easy.
But honey,
Living itself was tricky.
Using my emotions,
To protect myself.
While leaving you with the leftovers they had.
It wasn't easy to love you,
Drowning in my own poison,
Making you my doe eye audience.
Sacrificing your childhood,
To respect their adulthood.
Rejecting your curious mind,
Hurting your innocent heart.
Amidst all the verbal battles,
Forgive me for making you straddle.

12. I Remember

I remember,
Admiring your presence.
When you were working,
Being a son, they expected.
Missing out on,
Being a father, your's needed.
I understood your silence,
When you were lost in your game,
Leaving no room for me to blame.
I remember,
Being questioned by your presence,
Being your maid for 24/7,
But whenever I needed my husband,
Your unavailability was always excused.
I remember,
Being tortured by your presence,
When you were looking down on me,
My kids saw me as their parent,
Which you failed to be.
I have hated you for so many reasons,
Yet I chose to love you.
Not for the husband you were,
But for a decent human you were.

13. Pain became Aid

Come and see me laugh,
The way I used to.
Losing the glimpse of life,
While being your Housewife.
I have waited for so long,
To step in your shoe,
Just to see,
What it feels to be a mocker.
I get it,
You had to play your role,
Marking your duties.
While making me your Aid,
When I was reflecting your pain.
Years have passed,
Brown's still complimenting my beige,
Whilst mirrors are still the same,
Living under your name.
Only this time,
My shadow is far away dancing in the light.
When they saw,
Pain leaving his darkness,
To protect her kindness.

14. Flashbacks

Can I pack my bag?
Dreaming of a flashback.
Because life was perfect,
When we were nothing.
I wonder,
What would I be?
If not a Housewife.
All this time,
I kept blaming people around,
For something I became.
I kept blaming them,
For leaving my opinions,
When I left them long back.
I kept blaming them,
For walking all over me,
When I was the one,
Closing all the doors.
I kept blaming them,
For killing my emotions.
When I am the actual criminal.
I kept blaming them,
For my silence.
When I killed my own voice.
I wonder,

If I could go back in time,
Would I be any different?
I wonder,
If I could go back in time,
Would I still choose to be a housewife?

15. Tomorrow's

Afraid of tomorrow's,
Playfully ignoring the present.
Living in the past,
While dripping pain it reflected.
That's how she measured her life.
Every tomorrow enfolding a new chapter,
Coming from a background,
Where commitment is a duty.
Afraid of tomorrow's.
When she would become a hot topic.
When people were intruding her social life,
She was diving deep into a serious strife.
Terrified of becoming a wife,
But more so,
Petrified of becoming a societal housewife.
She was a women,
Afraid of tomorrow's.

16. Lawful Sister

Waking up to your presence,
From gossiping in our little kitchen,
To miss you on our own vacation.
You have been my partner,
More than my own husband ever has.
With the differences we had,
Time had something else planned.
From being two strangers,
We became the actual home owners.
Living in a house full of drama,
We both helped each other believe in karma.
They had eyes on our connection,
Accusing us of being two,
Robbing us from our relaxations,
You helped me reply with our meditation.
From dusk till dawn,
You made my ride easy enough,
To let their tantrums slide.
You entered as a sister-in-law,
While you ended up being my lawful sister.

17. A woman is a woman's______

Dedicated to My Woman.

Being a Woman,
You are a trusted enemy.
You are a trusted daughter,
Maybe a trusted wife.
But hardly a trusted friend.
Friendships are like an open cage.
You are either at an edge or at the same page.
That's a known theory,
Or that's what I thought,
Until I met her.
A line created by a society,
Relations became anxiety,
Living amongst the insanity,
She was a women,
Who made me realise my own capacity.
She was a woman,
Who taught me to embrace that line,
Changing the dynamics of society,
She became a woman,
Who made me believe in female friendships.
Being a woman,

Believe me,
You are only a human.
Mistakes made with your vulnerabilities,
Gives you more possibilities,
To drive back to the line with new responsibilities.
She was a woman,
Who made me believe in female abilities.
Being a woman,
She became my trusted human.

18. Have you Ever?

Have you ever knocked at her door,
How does she look?
On opening her door,
Do you think she is off the hook?
From formal meetings,
To informal greetings.
Living at a barrel age,
While finishing it with her preachings.
Have you ever looked at her?
Does she ever relax?
With all her work, career or home
Is it possible to keep her track?
A woman so full of herself,
Asking you for your help,
While ending up being occupied someplace else.
People often call her beauty with brains,
But have you seen her dancing through her pain.
Yes she can do it all,
But have you ever helped her,
When you see her fall?
You say you respect women,
Can you show me proof,
By not being one of those men.
Have you ever knocked at her door?

Because If you ever,

Can you keep your voice to your core?

19. Dear Society

Dear Society,
Just here to know
How is your anxiety?
I am curious enough,
To see how you feel,
Seeing a woman of your BG,
Now being recognised as an OG.
To tell you the truth,
She is inspiring your youth.
It's okay to dream,
She is the living proof.
Going away from your direction,
Dear Society,
How do you feel,
Realising she was never your reflection.
Rejecting your marital connections,
She ran away with her passion.
Dear Society,
How is your duplicity?
Trapped within your own complexity,
When she is owning up to her productivity.
I have a serious question to ask,
Will you banish her?
Simply on a choice she made,

To abandon your plan,
Recognising what she wants,
Knowing her, trust me,
She would do it all again.
Dear Society,
She was a woman of your society.
Now teaching your young ladies,
For its okay to have an Authority,
Rather than being Guilty.
Dear Society,
Just here to know,
How are you doing?
On seeing her growing.

20. Full Circle

Busking in sun,
Swinging on the porch,
Having a cup of coffee,
Made by my son.
Sitting at a dinner table filled with laughter,
When watching on screen shining bright, our daughter.
Things have changed,
Now there's no one to be blamed.
A housewife once soaked in her tears,
Is now working along with her peers.
Life has been a full circle,
A girl once walked alone in the sand,
Is now,
A woman walking with her family hand in hand.

21. Role Model

Housewife, A tag
A prestigious position,
A woman leading her home with ambition,
In a world full of this generation.
Where a woman like me,
Is scared to pursue this profession.
Led by a misconception,
Fueled with the contradictions,
Redeeming her marriage on set conditions,
Changing societal combinations.
Housewife, A tag,
A tag given,
In a society full of women so driven,
Overwhelmed by witnessing the barricade being broken,
Passionate to be outspoken.
Housewife, A tag,
Living in a world full of bars,
Coming out as a leading star,
Creating their own benchmark,
Giving an input, Donating their sparks.
Housewife, A tag
A real profession to brag.

www.ingramcontent.com/pod-product-compliance
Lightning Source LLC
LaVergne TN
LVHW010930200726
843509LV00013B/2152